Charles Woodruff Shields

The Order of the Sciences

An essay on the philosophical classification and organization of human knowledge

Charles Woodruff Shields

The Order of the Sciences
An essay on the philosophical classification and organization of human knowledge
ISBN/EAN: 9783337248529

Printed in Europe, USA, Canada, Australia, Japan

Cover: Foto ©Thomas Meinert / pixelio.de

More available books at **www.hansebooks.com**

THE ORDER OF THE SCIENCES

AN ESSAY

ON THE

PHILOSOPHICAL CLASSIFICATION AND ORGANIZATION
OF HUMAN KNOWLEDGE

BY

CHARLES W. SHIELDS

PROFESSOR IN PRINCETON COLLEGE

NEW YORK
CHARLES SCRIBNER'S SONS
1882

PREFACE.

The following essay includes the essential parts of a paper read before the Philosophical Society of Washington, together with some additional matter of an historical and critical nature, designed to render it a more complete monograph.

Whilst other classifications and schemes of science, which are before the public, such as those of Comte and Herbert Spencer, have been freely discussed, any sound principles upon which they proceed are carefully discriminated and retained, and the aim has been to complete them and advance beyond them to still remaining higher problems of philosophy, and contribute something toward their solution.

Princeton College,
May 22, 1882.

THE ORDER OF THE SCIENCES.

In one of the comedies of Molière, the philosopher is represented as becoming furious at the soldier for daring to call the profession of arms a science, instead of an art; and at another time, as posed in a quandary whether he should put hats in the category of figures or of fashions. So early had a passion for excessive classification become the butt of even dramatic satire.

And yet, that the subject has its grave as well as comic side, is shown by the fact that classifications of the arts and sciences have gone on multiplying in spite of repeated failures and a general incredulity, and that some of the greatest minds in modern times have been exercised upon the problem. There never was, in truth, more need of a right classification than at the present moment. As mere mental and social phenomena, the masses of human knowledge have become too vast and complex to be advantageously treated without some method and arrangement; while as intellectual pursuits they are so logically connected and interwoven, that no one of them can be intelligently cultivated without regard to the rest. Indeed, the ascertainment of the true normal order of the sciences is not merely a crying want in literature and in education, but is an essential part of the structure of science itself, without which it cannot be matured and completed. For " the sciences," said Bacon, " can as little grow apart as the branches severed from a common tree." And, accordingly, the most note-worthy attempts to supply this want have come of late from scientific thinkers and philosophers rather than from professional teachers and enclycopædists.

It is plain, moreover, that the classification now demanded must be something more than a mere artificial arrangement suggested by convenience and taste, and including only the superficial resemblances of one science with another. It must be real and essential, inhering in the sciences themselves, reflecting their actual relations and mutual dependencies, and exhibiting them as members of a logical organism, ra the than as mere gradual studies in a curriculum or alphabetical topics in a cyclopædia. And it must have acquired such scientific exactness and value that at length it shall be universally adopted to the exclusion of all other methods. In a word, it must be philosophical rather than pedagogical or encyclopediacal. It may be long before we shall see such a classification in use, but the time has at least come to offer schemes for consideration.

It would be a mistake to assume that such schemes must proceed from a mere pedantic love of method and system, and can be of no practical use and influence. Some of the worst evils of modern scientific controversy arise from the want of a lucid order on the part of otherwise clear and vigorous thinkers who have treated the sciences as mere *disjecta membra*, or through conceit and prejudice have forced them into false, confusing relations, which could not but lead to collision and conflict. The current disputes in respect to protoplasm, evolution, and agnosticism, are examples. And such evils are likely to continue until the bounds of the sciences have been rigorously defined, and their normal ranks and connections become so fixed and accepted, that border feuds and trespasses will no longer be possible. Nor should we forget the positive benefits which may accrue, not merely to learned societies, educational institutions and libraries, but to pure science itself, when we have ascertained the limits which separate our knowledge from our ignorance, and ensured a more economical division of labor among the investigators at work in different fields of research. The classification of sciences, according to Whewell, has its chief use in pointing out to us the extent of our powers of arriving at truth, and the analogies which obtain between the certain and lucid portions of knowledge and those other moral, political, and metaphysical portions which are not so advanced and perfect. Comte anticipated that a true gradation of the sciences, when in actual use, would regenerate education, both general and scientific; and Mr. Herbert Spencer agrees with him in thinking that through education it would have an immense effect upon civilization.

At the same time it would be very unwise to slight the difficulties of this important question. These are partly inherent in the vastness of its scope, and the multiplicity of its details; but they have also been greatly aggravated by the vague, conflicting senses in which scientific terms are employed. The problem, as stated by Comte, is to choose the one rational order out of a host of possible systems, as many as seven hundred and twenty being alternative to the one which he himself selected. "The difficulty of defining intimately connected studies," says Humboldt, " has been increased, because for centuries it has been customary to designate various branches of empirical knowledge by terms which admit either of too wide or too limited a definition of the ideas which they were intended to convey, and are, besides, objectionable from having had a different signification in those classical languages of antiquity from which they have been borrowed." The words physics, history, and philosophy, for example, have lost much of their original meaning, and become current in the most varied senses. And to this difficulty, it should be added, that the ground is already pre-occupied, not merely with conspicuous failures, but with more or less useful schemes of science, which have become traditional through long usage, and even illustrious by the great names associated with them.

If we recur to the history of the sciences, we shall find that their classification has varied with the advancement of exact knowledge, as well as with the caprices and fashions of philosophers.

At one time, whole sciences have been wanting in the existing scheme, merely because as yet they were unknown; at another time, well known sciences have been ignored or depreciated through some reigning prejudice; and at no time, until quite recently, have they been arranged with any approach to a philosophical order, from a strictly scientific motive. Indeed, such order as did obtain among them, was often implied rather than expressed, and can now only be discerned in the light of modern distinctions.

Among the early Greeks, after the mystical mathematics of Pythagoras, there would seem to have existed little more than a sort of crude speculative physics until the time of Socrates, who added the elements of logic and ethics.

Plato then wrought the existing mass of knowledge into the first comprehensive system, embracing in his dialectic a general science of cognition within which he included the special provinces of physics and ethics. Aristotle followed with his more precise delineation of logic as the organon or instrument of the sciences, which, by a masterly arrangement that has dominated the schools for centuries, he grouped into three great divisions, the Theoretical, the Practical, the Technical; the first including mathematics, physics, and metaphysics (primary philosophy or theology); the second including ethics, economics, and politics; and the third including technics, æsthetics, and rhetoric; theology as the head of the metaphysical realm being queen of the theoretical sciences, as the theoretical are themselves paramount to the practical and the technical.

The Stoics, whilst observing these divisions, re-arranged them on the principle that virtue is superior to knowledge, by subordinating theoretical to practical science, making logic ancillary to ethics, and merging theology in physics as a science of efficient and final causes.

The Epicureans, still further depreciating theoretical science, restricted logic to a search for the ethical canons of a happy life, and banished theology even from physics as wholly mythical and misleading.

And at length the Sceptics completed the debasement of pure science by involving it in a paradoxical logic and making it the highest aim of ethics to abstain from scientific inquiry.

Among the Romans, as little was added to the order as to the content of the sciences, Cicero in his philosophical writings having simply marshalled them in a rhetorical eclecticism, and the elder Pliny having industriously packed them away in his Natural History without any pretence of scientific method.

The Jewish and Christian schools of Alexandria, by a mystical theory of knowledge annexed the new domain of revealed theology to the ancient empire of Grecian science.

The Church fathers, whilst restoring theology

to her lost kingdom of metaphysics, with the exception of Augustine, depreciated and neglected the other sciences, though signs of a different tendency at length appeared in the encyclopædical works of Boëthius, Cassiodorus, Capella, and Alcuin, rival claimants for the time-honored scheme of the seven liberal arts and studies.

But it was reserved for the Scholastics of the middle ages to render theology queen of all the sciences, both theoretical and practical, physical and metaphysical, by making the entire academic course, with its trivium (grammar, rhetoric, logic) and quadrivium (music, arithmetic, geometry, astronomy), a mere preparation for the study of divinity, like the pedagogic by which Grecian and Roman youths had formerly been trained for the service of the State. The cyclopædia or circle of the sciences, arranged in the Aristotelian order, was closed within the pale of the Church, and philosophy scarcely allowed a place outside the theological curriculum.

The exceptions were such enlightened doctors as Roger Bacon, who projected a scheme of universal knowledge in his Compendium of Philosophy; Vincent of Beauvais, whose Fourfold Mirror of History, Nature, Morals and Doctrine reflected the entire range of mediæval learning; and Gregory Reisch, whose Margarita Philosophica or Epitome of every kind of Science, constituted, according to Humboldt, the first great encyclopædia from which to date the modern attempts to classify the various branches of knowledge.

It was, however, not until the Reformers had fully liberated philosophy in the act of emancipating theology, that Descartes led forth the metaphysical sciences, and Bacon the physical sciences, into widening fields of research with ever growing harvests of truth. The result is, that for three centuries the different groups of sciences, having become independent, not merely of theology, but of one another, have been contending over their boundaries—sometimes for dominion, sometimes for existence, the physical with the mental, both with the metaphysical, and at times all with the theological—like the rival European sovereignties which meanwhile were striving to maintain or extend their discovered possessions in the new world. But at length, with the complete map of the globe, we may begin to look for a complete map of science, and already attempt what Bacon finely calls "a general and faithful perambulation of learning, with an inquiry what parts thereof lie fresh and waste, and not improved by the industry of man."

It becomes evident from this glance at the history of the sciences, that the problem of their coördination belongs to an advanced period of their development, and can only be solved by the combined and successive attempts of many laborers. Each of the sciences must at least have found a name and a place in human estimation, in order that all the classifiable objects may be fully before us; and even then it would be the height of presumption and conceit to imagine that by one stroke of genius they could be marshalled into perfect order. Not only must we begin with an unprejudiced survey of the whole existing mass of scientific knowledge, but we must patiently examine the classifications of our predecessors, carefully weigh their merits and defects, cull out the sound principles which have survived their failures, and combine them with any we have to contribute, and then be content to regard our own favorite scheme as still but tentative and approximate—in short, we must pursue the same modest experimental method by which we arrive at all scientific truth. We shall do well to continually keep in mind the lesson which history plainly teaches, that it is only in and by the progress of the sciences themselves that their true classification can be brought into view, and that all other classifications which we may seek to impose upon them, will be swept aside as antiquated rubbish, the mere scaffolding and waste-material of a structure of which they could form no part.

At the outset, we need a simple definition of science: not a precise, metaphysical definition, such as might be reached by only a few minds after much thought, and such as will more fittingly emerge at a later stage of this investigation, but a leading conception naturally suggested by the existing body of scientific knowledge. The word itself, as derived from *scire*, to know, may serve as such a starting point. Science is knowledge, exact knowledge, or acquaintance with facts, which are the real stuff of knowledge, distinguishing it from faith and from fancy, which do not always involve facts, or may involve error and fiction with them. We may believe or imagine what does not exist, but we can be said to know only what really is. Men have believed, for example, that the planets forecast our fortunes, or have imagined them performing a choral dance in their orbits; but such superstition or poetry does not belong to that portion of exact knowledge termed astronomy.

And yet all exact knowledge is not science. There is an animal instinct, or a human sagacity which, within limits, is precise and certain without being scientific. The unreasoning bee builds and stores its cell upon mechanical and chemical principles, and the untaught sailor has a weather-wisdom which puzzles the meteorologist. But such intuitive intelligence does not constitute the reasoned and approved knowledge which multitudes have tested and handed down through successive generations under the names of chemistry and physics.

There is also a character of generality in scientific knowledge. It not only embraces observed facts without any admixture of fiction, but it embraces them in their actual connections, as generalized under the laws or uniformities of their co-existence and succession. If there be a popular wisdom, a traditional acquaintance with many natural laws and causes, which has become crudely condensed in maxims and usages, yet these are very different from the systematic bodies of knowledge which are found in the physical and some of the mental and social sciences.

Other features of science might be discussed, such as its power of prevision, its cumulative tests, its disinterested aims, its superiority to human prejudices and vicissitudes, its dignity and utility; but for the present purpose it may be sufficiently defined as exact, verified, systematic knowledge of facts. If this general definition be correct, we must at once eliminate certain adjuncts and products of the sciences, which are often confounded with them, but which ought not to be admitted into a strictly philosophical classification.

In the first place, it is important that the sciences should be distinguished from the various branches of mere *Learning*, which is but the vehicle and ornament of science. The languages and literatures of different nations, as mastered by the scholar, may contain and propagate a vast amount of scientific knowledge, but viewed apart from their content and purport, they cannot themselves assume a scientific form until they have been made the proper subject of philology and the related sciences that deal with the origin and growth of dialects, races, and arts. In like manner, History, though susceptible of a scientific character, is commonly treated as a mere branch of literature or rhetoric.

In the second place, the sciences should also be distinguished from the *Arts*, which are but the applications and aids of science. The industrial arts, such as Navigation, Engineering, Metallurgy, Agriculture, Manufactures, are sometimes loosely called practical sciences, or bread-and-butter sciences, because pursued for a livelihood rather than for the increase of pure knowledge; and this discrimination is justified by the fact that they were for ages practiced, and may still be practiced by the mere artisan, without much acquaintance with the mechanical and chemical sciences to which they are related, and upon which their greatest advancement depends. The æsthetical arts, such as Architecture, Sculpture, Painting, Music, Oratory, Poetry, do indeed aim at the beautiful rather than the useful, but they have been mastered by some of the greatest artists, not only in advance, but in ignorance of the corresponding physical and mental sciences whose business it is to evolve the principles that are involved in every work of art and product of the imagination. And even the ethical arts, such as the learned professions of Law, Medicine, and Divinity, though they presuppose a liberal education in all the sciences, and require the highest moral aims in the practitioner, cannot claim the properly scientific spirit and character, inasmuch as they simply apply knowledge, rather than accumulate it for its own sake.

In the third place, the sciences should still further be distinguished from the disciplinal *Studies*, which are but the instruments and processes of science. In the trivium of the schools, Grammar, Rhetoric, and Logic were termed the three arts of discourse, and have ever been valued as a training and equipment of the intellectual powers, more than for any positive knowledge which they involve. Logic, as the science of thought, is simply a branch of psychology, while, as the art of reasoning, it may properly prescribe the various methods of scientific investigation. Mathematics also is a pure science of ideas and ideal relations, rather than of observed facts and laws, until it becomes mixed with the real sciences, when it appears as a higher kind of applied logic, the sciences becoming exact in proportion as they can be made to assume a mathematical expression. And Metaphysics, the science of existence, as we shall see further on, is rather a species or general division of science than one of the sciences themselves, while as a dialectical study it serves to discipline the powers of abstraction, generalization and comparison, which are needed in them all.

In the fourth place, all the other sciences may finally be distinguished from *Philosophy*, which is at once the science and the art of the sciences. That much abused word is indeed used in various senses. Sometimes it is restricted to psychology, or mental science, in distinction from all physical science. Sometimes it is confounded with metaphysics, as when we speak of the philosophy of nature or the philosophy of religion. Sometimes it traverses both psychology and metaphysics, as when we speak of the idealistic philosophy, the positive philosophy, the transcendental philosophy. Sometimes it is made equivalent to logic, as when we speak of the inductive philosophy, or the philosophy of the inductive sciences. And sometimes it becomes a name for science in general with its various divisions, as when we speak of natural philosophy, mental philosophy, political philosophy, and religious philosophy. But there is no good reason why it should not consistently include all these senses, as being that one comprehensive science of the sciences, which must embrace both physics and metaphysics, together with the mathematics and logic involved in their construction. In this full meaning of the word, philosophy may be said to contain the whole of the sciences, while no one of the sciences, not even theology, can be said to contain the whole of philosophy.

The distinctions which we are urging, may be exhibited to the eye in a tabular form, by placing together some examples of classifiable sciences, though as yet in no definite order, preceded by some of the studies which serve as their appliances, and followed by some of the arts in which they are themselves practically applied.

THE ORDER OF THE SCIENCES. 21

APPLIANCES OF SCIENCE. CLASSIFIABLE SCIENCES. APPLICATIONS OF SCIENCE.

Letters.	Studies.	Astronomy.	Useful Arts.	Fine Arts.
Latin.	Grammar.	Chemistry.	Navigation.	Painting.
Greek.	Rhetoric.	Psychology.	Agriculture.	Music.
Modern Languages.	Logic.	Physics.	Metallurgy.	Sculpture.
Belles Lettres.	Mathematics.	Biology.	Economics.	Poetry.
Historiography.	Dialectics.	Sociology.	Manufactures.	Architecture.

It need scarcely be said that we are not disparaging the various branches of literature, the practical arts, and the scholastic studies, by thus distinguishing them from the positive sciences with which they are more or less connected, and often confounded. In the scheme of an encyclopædia, it would be right to include all the former with the latter; and in the scale of a curriculum, it might even be proper to place some of the former higher than the latter, according as they were to be pursued in a school of letters, or in a school of the arts, or in a professional school of law, medicine, or divinity; only in a school of science or philosophy would they take a lower rank.

The question of the relative worth and dignity of human pursuits is not here before us. All that we now seek is to fix the sense in which words are to be used, by insisting that in a philosophical scheme of the sciences should be included only those bodies of ascertained knowledge which remain distinct and peculiar, though they may be expressed in elegant literature, applied in the useful arts, constructed by means of the disciplinal studies, and at length logically organized in philosophy.

In the light of these definitions and distinctions we may now intelligently examine some of the leading classifications which have been proposed. We need not stop to notice the numerous schemes from Aristotle down to Locke, based upon the ethical distinction between theoretical and practical knowledge, nor the countless projects for correlating the sciences with various interests which they subserve, such as the ecclesiastical division into sciences of authority, sciences of reason, and sciences of observation; the civil classification of Leibnitz, according to the learned faculties and professions; the academic classification of Jeremy Bentham as pedantically set forth in his " Chrestomathia," for the instruction of the higher classes; and the bibliographical classification of Roswell Park, whose " Pantology " was designed to furnish courses of reading in all the sciences and arts, arranged in the form of an encyclopediacal tree. The so-called practical sciences, or moral and useful arts, having been already precluded by our definitions, we pass at once to such classifications as are more strictly philosophical in their aim.

Without attempting the excessive refinement

of a classification of classifications, we shall find it important to observe that they are of two sorts, the subjective and the objective; those adjusted to our internal faculties, and those adjusted to external realities; those proceeding upon the order of ideas in man, and those proceeding upon the order of facts in nature.

First among the former appears the comprehensive scheme employed by Bacon in the "Advancement of Learning," and afterwards adopted by Dalembert in the celebrated French Encyclopædia, and by Baron Bielfield, of Prussia, in his "Elements of Universal Erudition." It proceeded upon the psychological principle of adjusting the sciences to the mental faculties which severally produce them, and are the fountains of knowledge in the human mind: History relating to the memory, Poetry to the imagination, and Philosophy to the reason; the first division embracing Civil, Ecclesiastical, and Natural History with the Mechanic Arts; the second division (as amended by Dalembert) embracing Lyric, Epic, and Dramatic Poetry, with the Fine Arts; and the third division embracing Natural Philosophy, both physical and metaphysical, Human Philosophy, both individual and social, and Divine Philosophy, or Theology, both natural and revealed. The beautiful symmetry displayed through all the numerous subdivisions of this scheme and its rhetorical convenience for an encyclopediacal treatment of the different branches of human learning have been often and justly praised, but as a strictly scientific arrangement of strictly scientific knowledge, it has been almost rendered obsolete by the advancement of modern science, as well as by the searching criticism to which it has been subjected. Dugald Stewart, in particular, in his preface to the "Encyclopædia Britannica" has shown that its analysis of the mental faculties is incomplete, as it does not include the powers of abstraction and generalization; that memory, imagination, and reason, instead of being always separately exercised, are often blended in intellectual pursuits; and that consequently in such an arrangement the sciences and arts are confused together under the same general titles, as for example, metaphysics with astronomy, and the mechanic arts with civil history.

Upon the same subjective principle proceeded the elaborate scheme devised by the poet-philosopher, Coleridge, and adopted by the editors of the " Encyclopædia Metropolitana," with the view of more strictly separating the scientific from the literary and historical material of learning, and blending a philosophical with the usual alphabetical treatment of such topics. It was based upon the Kantian psychology; the Pure Sciences issuing from the pure reason and dealing only with the ideas and acts of the mind in itself, and the Mixed Sciences issuing from the sensuous understanding and dealing with observed phenomena, as combined with abstract principles: the former being subdivided (1) into the Formal Sciences, grammar, rhetoric, logic, and mathematics, and (2) the Real Sciences, metaphysics, ethics, and theology; and the latter being subdivided into (1) Experimental Sciences, such as mechanics, hydrostatics, optics, and (2) Applied Sciences, or the the useful and fine arts. The authors of this ingenious classification avowed high moral and didactic motives; but however serviceable it may have proved for their purpose, it must be objected to it, as to the scheme of Bacon, that it involves psychological distinctions which are not sufficiently precise or generally accepted. In regard to all such schemes, indeed, it may be questioned whether psychology, even if it were perfected, would not be too narrow a basis for the whole superstructure of the sciences. There would seem to be no natural or essential connection among them, if they are to be separately conjoined with the different mental faculties which produce them, and thus artificially arranged as mere pursuits of the human intellect.

A more logical application of the subjective principle, also on the basis of the Kantian metaphysics, was afforded by Dr. Whewell in his comprehensive work on the Philosophy of the Sciences. Instead of adjusting them to the mental faculties, he sought to arrange them in accordance with the fundamental ideas or conceptions upon which they proceed: mathematics proceeding upon the ideas of space, time, and number; mechanics upon the additional ideas of force and motion; chemistry upon the ideas of affinity and likeness; biology upon the ideas of life and final cause; psychology upon the ideas of emotion and thought; the palætiological sciences upon the idea of historical cause; and natural theology upon the idea of the First Cause; each following science involving also the ideas of its predecessor. In favor of this profound and beautiful arrangement, it may be urged that it is the result of an historical and philosophical study of the sciences themselves, pursued with wonderful breadth and acuteness of view; that it rigidly distinguishes the theoretical sciences from the practical arts; and that it exhibits them as concatenated in an intelligible, if not strictly logical order. Its defects are that it avowedly foregoes any complete classification of the mental and social sciences; that it largely ignores the objective materials or facts of knowledge for the sake of the ideas that mould and combine them; and that it runs out into metaphysical questions, concerning which practical men of science are not likely to be soon agreed.

It has been wittily said of Whewell, that science was his forte and omniscience his foible; but the logical principle of his classification found its extravagant climax in another philosopher, whose fancied omniscience was based upon a scorn of real science. The encyclopædia of Hegel was consistently framed in accordance with his panlogistic philosophy. Assuming that whatever is, is rational, that even nature is but petrified logic, and dialectic the process of re-thinking the whole thought of the Creator, he essayed by mere syllogistic reasoning, and without any aid from experience, to build up a purely ideal series of sciences; beginning with logic as the science of abstract thought, thence rising through the concrete notions successively emerging in the natural sciences, mechanics, physics, organics, and thence ascending through the more complex conceptions of the mental sciences, ethics, politics, and religion, towards the fulness of the absolute idea in philosophy, embracing thus the totality of existence, from zero to infinity, in one concatenated process.

Of this subtle and brilliant construction it may be said that it has proved at once the boast of the metaphysician and the scandal of the scientist. On the one hand, it is claimed as the most comprehensive scheme of human knowledge that has ever been devised, and one that all future research must verify, and it certainly is well adapted to the literary purposes of a complete encyclopædia. But, on the other hand, it sins against the first law of true science, by assuming that a preconceived order of thoughts in our minds must be identical with the actual order of things in nature, and then, at every step, so blends the metaphysical with the empirical realms of inquiry as to be practically worthless for any strictly scientific purpose. It may only serve to illustrate conclusively the risk and absurdity of attempting to arrange the sciences solely with reference to the human faculties or conceptions which they involve, and without any regard to those external realities and relations upon which they are founded, and in accordance with which primarily they should be adjusted.

In passing now to the opposite principle of classification, we should observe that it is difficult to find a pure example of either method. Some of the examples already cited are not wholly wanting in the elements of a more natural and scientific arrangement. Bacon, in subdividing the sciences that proceed from the reason, grouped them in three great provinces of reality, nature, man, and God, as natural, human, and divine sciences; and Coleridge, even among his sciences of the pure reason, distinguished the real from the formal, while his mixed sciences, issuing from the understanding, were projected in the external world of phenomena. In like manner we shall see in the examples that are to follow, that the objective or empirical principle has not always been exclusively and consistently applied, and it will still be our task to sift the true from the false, until we get all the needed data for a final judgment.

A first step toward a sound classification was taken by Dugald Stewart, when, in opposition to the Baconian scheme, he suggested the two realms of Mind and Matter as chief divisions of philosophy, the former to include the Intellectual, Ethical, and Political sciences, and the latter the Mathematical and Natural sciences. Without starting the metaphysical question between the spiritualist and the materialist, all parties will agree that physical and psychical phenomena, with their corresponding sciences, are clearly distinguishable. And a further advance was afterwards made by Neil Arnott, when he arranged these two sets of sciences in a pyramidal series, rising from physics to ethics, and again by Patrick Dove, whose theory of human progression towards a universal reign of justice was based upon the supposed order in which the seriate sciences come to effect in corresponding arts.

But the constructive, systematizing genius of the French seems to have afforded the most fruitful soil for the growth of these principles. Descartes led the way with his aphorism, first broached in the physics of Aristotle, that our knowledge proceeds from things easily learned to those more difficult, from the simple to the complex, from the general to the special; and a host of ingenious classifications followed. Prominent among them, was the elaborate scheme projected by the French physicist, Ampère, and bequeathed as his last scientific attainment. It was entitled a "Natural classification of all Human Knowledge," having resulted from an empirical study of the sciences themselves, and was based upon the classificatory principle by which naturalists arrange objects in kingdoms, genera, and species. The two most general divisions or kingdoms were the cosmological sciences of nature, and the noological sciences of mind. The former comprised the two sub-kingdoms of inanimate objects and animate objects. Each of these again branched into two sections, which were in their turn bisected, and this bifurcate division, which according to Ampère inheres in the nature of things, was thus carried through six distinct orders of fact, in both the natural and the mental world, until as many as one hundred and twenty-eight sciences and arts had been enumerated, with appropriate technical names. The artificial symmetry and prolixity of this scheme, its cumbrous new-coined nomenclature, and its mixture of the arts with the sciences, would have been a bar to its adoption, as they may have been to a fair discussion of its merits. It contained, however, some valuable distinctions, which still figure in the most recent systems, and in particular, the principle upon which Ampère insisted, that the sciences ought not to be studied in vicious circles, one ever recurring into another, but according to the serial order in which he had tabulated them.

A contemporary critic, Cournot, in an "Essay on the Foundations of the Sciences," endeavored to combine the principles of Bacon and Ampère in a scheme which was also professedly founded upon reality, both relative and absolute, and for the mental faculties substituted certain social temperaments or stages, through which human knowledge is supposed to have advanced in space and time, from its crude state in religion and art, towards the perfect scientific character. These gradations were termed History, Philosophy, and Science; the first embracing such subdivisions as geography and civil history; the second, such subdivisions as mythology and theology or metaphysics; and the third, the arts and theoretical sciences. The theoretical sciences were then arranged in a series, ascending from the simple to the complex, and comprising the mathematical, the physical, the biological, the noological, and the political sciences. Among the advocates of this system was Isidore Saint Hilaire, and the historical principle which it involved, though it complicated the tabular arrangement, was undoubtedly a step in the right direction.

It remained for Auguste Comte, a contemporary of Ampère and Cournot, to embody the merits of these systems with but few of their defects, in his acute and luminous treatise termed "The Philosophy of the Positive Sciences." Restricting science itself to an empirical study of facts and their laws, excluding theology and metaphysics as a mere unscientific search for causes, separating the positive sciences from the arts, and still further distinguishing the abstract from the concrete sciences, Comte then proceeded to arrange the abstract sciences, which he had thus obtained, according to the interdependent phenomena to which they refer, in the order of their decreasing generality and simplicity. All natural philosophy was first divided into inorganic physics and organic physics, corresponding to the two most general classes of phenomena. The former was then subdivided into celestial physics or astronomy, both geometrical and mechanical, and terrestrial physics, both mechanical and chemical. Organic physics was also subdivided into biology, the science of organisms, both vegetal and animal, and sociology, the science of associated organisms, both animal and human. Five fundamental sciences were thus arranged, all of them physical or natural sciences. Psychology, as distinct from biology, was not allowed a place. But a sixth science, mathematics, the most abstract study of the simplest and most general of all facts, was made the foundation and source of the whole ascending series of sciences, as being itself independent of them, whilst all of them are more or less dependent upon it. Astronomy, the next in order, though directly dependent upon mathematics, is largely independent of terrestrial physics by reason of the greater generality and simplicity of its data, the heavens ever affecting the earth, but the earth scarcely affecting the heavens. Terrestrial physics, chemistry, biology, then follow in the scale of increasing dependence and complexity, until we reach the summit in social physics, where the phenomena became so mixed and multiform as hitherto to have defied scientific investigation.

In favor of this so-called hierarchy of the sciences, Comte ingeniously argued that it is the order which the sciences themselves have spontaneously assumed, as separately pursued, without any effort to arrange them; that it coincides with their actual historical succession, astronomy having long preceded the later-born sciences of physics and chemistry; and also that it verifies his own law of their intellectual evolution, from the theological through the metaphysical into the positive state of exact knowledge; mathematics and astronomy having already become the most positive of the sciences, because most remotely connected with humanity and least exposed to theological and metaphysical perversion, whilst biology and social physics, being in the thick of human passions and interests, are still enveloped in primitive superstition and mysticism. To these arguments, Comte added the practical consideration that his gradation of the sciences is the only logical order in which they can be successfully taught and studied in schools of general or scientific culture.

The fascinating simplicity of this scheme, its logical convenience, and the large amount of truth which it contains, caused it for a time to pass unchallenged in the scientific world, until at length it became the centre of a wide controversy among the leading philosophers of the age. The most varied views have been taken of its general principles and of its details. On the one side, Dr. Whewell, in defence of his own ideal scheme, resisted the attempt to banish metaphysics and theology from the realm of science, as not warranted by the history of physical discovery, and in itself a pedantic and capricious limitation of our knowledge, to which the intellect of man neither can nor should submit. Professor Huxley, in his trenchant manner, remarked that metaphysics was with Comte a general term of offence for whatever he did not like, and that the sciences, instead of being like steps in a ladder, are but branches from the common stem of molecular physics. Mr. Herbert Spencer, in vindication of his own originality as well as in opposition to the whole Comtean classification, more directly assailed its distinctive principles, maintaining that its serial arrangement of the sciences, though requisite for literary purposes, has no basis either in nature or in history, since phenomena never occur logically, least of all in the supposed hierarchical order, and because the sciences have been simultaneous rather than successive in their progress; the simple depending upon the complex as well as the complex upon the simple; astronomy alone having owed at least ten important discoveries to the later physics and chemistry. Professor John Fiske, of Harvard, one of the most discriminating critics of the system, united with Mr. Spencer in showing that Comte had strangely mixed up the abstract with the concrete sciences in his hierarchy; mathematics, physics, and chemistry with astronomy, biology, and sociology; and that the true historic order of their succession is spiral rather than linear, being not alone due to the relative generality of phenomena, but also and much more largely due to their relative conspicuousness, their frequency, their concreteness and the varying means of investigating them. While both critics were thus agreed in renouncing the serial principle as worthless, they further argued that the whole metaphysical region, which Comte had simply ignored, must in the nature of the case be unknowable.

On the other side of the debate appeared Mr. Lewes, whose "Biographical History of Philosophy" was written to prove that theology and metaphysics have for centuries been steadily retreating before the march of the Positive Philosophy, and who accepted "its luminous conception of a new and final classification of the sciences as evincing a gigantic force of philosophic thought." Professor Bain also virtually adopted it in his Logic. M. Littré, the most distinguished French disciple of Comte, besides defending the originality of his master from the attacks of the English critics, replied that the true normal order of the sciences may be observed in their constitutions, and still holds objectively in things in accordance with the increasing complexity of phenomena, howsoever it may be reversed and confused in our minds by the abstracting and generalizing faculties. Mr. John Stuart Mill, by far the ablest and most judicious exponent of the system, also stood with Littré for its defence, maintaining that at least it served its purpose as a logically convenient arrangement, and that it is historically true, not, indeed, that one of the sciences has been finished before another was begun, but that they have proceeded together towards perfection at unequal rates in the order of their difficulty, the simple ever in advance of the complex, though with mutual aid and acceleration; and moreover that the alleged mixture of the concrete with the abstract sciences is but a verbal objection, astronomy or celestial physics being an abstract as well as concrete science. The French and the English defender of Comte were not only thus united in retaining the serial principle as essential, but also in abstaining from any metaphysical speculation as to the ultimate limits of knowledge.

As the outcome of this controversy we now have another classification, proposed by Mr. Spencer, and amended by Mr. Fiske, which in place of a linear series of ascending ranks, would substitute three collateral groups of sciences, one distinguishable from another according to the degree of their logical abstractness: the Abstract Sciences, the Abstract-Concrete Sciences, and the Concrete Sciences; the first to include sciences of ideal relations, viewed apart from all facts, such as logic and mathematics; the second to include sciences of real relations, implicated in certain classes of facts, such as mechanics, physics, and chemistry; and the third to include sciences of aggregated facts, involving both ideal and real relations, such as astronomy, geology, and biology. These groups, though not to be put in a serial order, are further defined as instrumental with respect to one another, the first with respect to the second and third, and the second with respect to the third only, while they furnish material to one another in an inverse order, the third to the second, and the second and third to the first. Each great group of sciences, moreover, is to be divided into numerous sub-groups, on the same principle of logical abstractness and universality.

Mr. Fiske, in adopting the classification of Mr. Spencer, has condensed and re-stated it, so that the Abstract Sciences, dealing with relations that are qualitative and quantitative, shall include logic and mathematics; the Abstract-Concrete sciences, dealing with properties that are manifested in masses and molecules, shall include molar physics, molecular physics and chemistry; and the Concrete Sciences, dealing with aggregates as actually exemplified in the heavens, in the earth, and in living organisms, shall include astronomy, geology, biology, psychology and sociology. Into each one of these five concrete sciences he would introduce a sub-division, referring to the evolution of phenomena from an ancient to the present condition; astrogeny, dealing with the genesis of the stellar and planetary systems; geogeny, dealing with the genesis of our globe; biogeny, dealing with the genesis of species; psycogeny, with the genesis of mental faculties and feelings; and sociogeny, with the genesis of moral and political institutions. Both of these distinguished thinkers were agreed in substituting for the linear procession of the sciences a complex spiral movement of combined analysis and synthesis, the concrete sciences ever reacting upon the abstract, and the abstract ever stimulating the concrete.

The elegance and perspicuity of this scheme have been justly praised, and as far as it goes, its general accuracy and logical serviceableness need not be questioned. But it has been incisively remarked by Mr. Stuart Mill, that it is an attempt to classify the sciences, not according to their subject matter or mutual relations, but according to an unimportant difference in the manner in which we come to know them; or, as Mr. Spencer himself expresses it, according to the order in which they may be built up in the human consciousness. In other words, it retains a shred of the vicious subjective method, upon which we have already animadverted, being to some extent an ideal arrangement, based upon our modes of knowing, rather than upon things known: and although as such, it may be true and useful, yet to marshal the sciences merely with reference to our logical convenience in cultivating them, would seem to be no more philosophical than to arrange them with reference to their ethical value, or their rhetorical symmetry, or their practical importance. Moreover, it should be observed that Mr. Fiske, whilst avowedly rejecting the serial principle, has implicitly re-admitted it into his group of concrete sciences, by adjusting them to the evolutionary succession of phenomena. After all that may be said in praise of this latest and best scheme, it does not seem likely that it will be accepted as complete and final; and the problem still remains, by a more careful analysis, to reject the discovered errors, and combine the residual truths of previous systems.

In now attempting this difficult problem, we shall pursue the method of successively enunciating the principles of a sound philosophical classification, and applying them, as far as possible, to the existing state of scientific knowledge; premising that the full force of these principles will better appear from a combined view of them, than from a separate estimate of any one of them, and least of all, of the one first to be stated.

I. *A philosophical scheme of the sciences should be based upon the facts which support them, rather than upon the ideas which they involve.*

It is not meant that the most concrete sciences do not involve ideas and ideal relations, nor yet that the most abstract sciences may not be evolved from facts as actually connected, but simply, that inasmuch as facts afford the foundation and material of knowledge, the order of facts, if it can be ascertained, should be allowed to determine the order of the sciences which are built upon them. While there may be some truth and much convenience in ideal classifications, yet being ideal and not empirical, they may have been largely preconceived in advance of experience, and in using them we shall be in danger of imposing upon facts an artificial arrangement of our own which they will not bear, and thus driving the sciences into false and hurtful connections. But when we shall have discovered the distinctions and relations which actually obtain among facts, there will then be revealed to us the solid foundations upon which to begin to erect the whole superstructure of real knowledge.

A strict application of this principle would exclude the abstract sciences of Logic and Mathematics from a philosophical classification, and retain them as disciplinal studies, until by being employed in empirical investigations, they acquire a content of positive knowledge, when they simply become parts and processes of other more real sciences. And in this view of their aim and scope, the chief authorities are substantially agreed, with the exception of the few German metaphysicians, such as Hegel and Oken, who have held that logic is the essential science of nature, and mathematics the original and substantial framework of the universe. Indeed, for the same reason, the whole distinction between the abstract and the concrete sciences, being one that is in our thoughts rather than in things, may be disregarded, and the two condensed into a single series to be simply termed FUNDAMENTAL SCIENCES, based upon actual relations which obtain among facts. We proceed to complete a list of such sciences by the aid of the next principle.

II. *A philosophical scheme of the sciences should fully reflect all the distinct classes of facts which have been scientifically ascertained.*

As the important distinctions among facts do not lie patent on the face of nature, but are to be learned in the progress of science itself, it follows that the right classification of the sciences must proceed with their own development, as one set of phenomena after another is distinguished and subjected to scientific methods, until the circle of known and knowable facts is complete. And no classification can be complete which ignores any such group of phenomena. It would be as unphilosophical to exclude a class of facts from mere dislike of them, or through some prejudice against investigating them, as it would be to include mere abstractions or notions for which one may have a fancy. The aim should be to admit every group of phenomena which nature presents for investigation, and which science has clearly brought into view as regulated by laws, even though those laws may not have been ascertained, and as yet seem scarcely ascertainable. For we are not to measure the uniformity of nature by the degree of precision in our knowledge of it; and history warns us that it would be rash to declare any class of facts too complex, remote, or recondite to be ever mastered by the processes of science.

Applying this principle, we may begin with the general obvious distinction between material facts and mental facts, as affording ground for the two chief groups of the *physical* and the *psychical* sciences. Let it be observed that this is not necessarily a metaphysical distinction. We here abstain from any inquiry into the essential nature of matter or mind. You may hold that they are two diverse substances, or that mind is a mere form of matter, or matter a mere form of mind, or both mere modes of some third inscrutable essence or force. In either or any case the distinction will still appear in phenomena themselves, viewed apart from any deeper foundation which it may or may not have in the ontological region beneath them. And it is a distinction which has been so universally accepted that we cannot speak in any language without recognizing it, however little practical importance some may attach to it. When, therefore, Comte would have arbitrarily ignored this distinction, and merged the mental, moral, and political sciences in physics, he simply confused classes of facts, which are at least as distinguishable as mechanical from chemical, or chemical from vital phenomena. And in this attempt to obliterate a whole group of sciences, he has not by any means been followed by his own disciples, not even by those who take a materialistic view of mental processes, still less by such critics as Lewes and Spencer. Even Stuart Mill, though adopting the Comtean hierarchy, is careful to amend it by inserting psychology between biology and sociology, insisting that mental phenomena, with their laws already so largely ascertained, afford material for a distinct and independent science, however intimately connected it may be with the neighboring regions of physiology and sociology. But when he adds that with the prospective establishment of sociology among the sciences "the circle of human knowledge will be complete, and it can only thereafter receive further enlargement by perpetual expansion from within," he seems not to have observed or remembered that there is still another class of facts quite as distinct as mental or social facts, though largely implicated with them, and quite as susceptible, it may be, of scientific investigation. Indeed, a surmise of their scientific character may be said to have long ago appeared in certain philosophers having no professional interest in them, such as Machiavelli, St. Simon, Hume, who have sought to construct a natural history of religion. Mr. Mill himself has suggested, in his last work, that the doctrines of religion should be treated as scientific theorems, to be tested like any of the speculative conclusions of physical science. M. Emile Burnouf claims to have founded a science of religions upon comparative ethnology, with good hopes of determining the laws of their evolution. And we have the authority of a distinguished philologist, Professor Max Müller, for retaining in this field of research the time-honored name of Theology, Comparative and Theoretic Theology. It is true, Professor Müller doubts whether the common classification of religions as natural and revealed, will any longer serve the purposes of science; but that is a question partly empirical and partly metaphysical, which can only be settled by the proper scientific methods. Whatever views may be taken of the origin and essential basis of religious phenomena, whether the subjective and the objective factors in their production are homogeneous or heterogeneous, the phenomena themselves cannot be questioned, both the new school of comparative theologians and the old school of professional divines being now agreed, though from different stand-points, in treating such phenomena scientifically. Nor can it be doubted that with the admission of theology among the empirical sciences, the only remaining class of facts is compassed, and the circle of human knowledge becomes complete.

It appears, therefore, that the progress of science has brought into view six distinct classes of facts, affording ground for as many corresponding groups of fundamental sciences: the Physical, the Chemical, the Organical, the Psychical, the Social, and the Religious. Each of these groups will be found to have several divisions, more or less distinct, according to the degree of its advancement towards the perfect scientific character. Physical Science embraces Molar Physics or Mechanics, dealing with material masses at rest and in motion; and Molecular Physics, dealing with the molecular undulations or ethereal vibrations of sound, heat, light, electricity and galvanism. Chemical Science embraces Inorganic Chemistry, dealing with the combination of atoms or elements in definite proportions; and Organic Chemistry, dealing with the re-composition of molecules in organized bodies. Organical or Biological Science embraces Botany, dealing with the different orders of plants, from the fungus up to the oak; and Zoology, dealing with the different orders of animals, from the mollusk up to man, the flower and head of organic nature, with his varied races, languages and arts. Psychical Science embraces Psychical Statics, dealing with the nervous functions and mental faculties, the senses, the intellect and the will; and Psychical Dynamics, dealing with the laws of mental processes in sensation, thought and emotion. Social Science embraces Social Statics, dealing with the organization of individuals into the family, the state and humanity; and Social Dynamics, dealing with the laws of social evolution from barbarism to civilization. Religious Science embraces Comparative Theology, dealing with the great ethnic and general religions; and Theoretic Theology, dealing with the development of essential or absolute religion.

It will be seen, by a glance at this scheme, that while the physical sciences have obtained a large degree of fullness and precision, the psychical sciences are still somewhat crude and indistinct: but the recent history of the latter already proves their analogy with the former. In mental science there has been a steady progress since the elder Mill began to formulate the laws of association among ideas. In social science, from the time of Vico, we have been growing familiar with the laws of historic recurrence and average progress, evolution through revolution, advanced individuals stimulating society, and advanced society still carrying forward individuals in ever ascending stages of civilization. And even in religious science Bishop Butler long ago threw out the bold conjecture that the entire history of the Christian scheme of redemption, with all its miraculous phenomena, if viewed by an adequate intelligence, would appear as much regulated by general laws as the march of the seasons or the growth of a flower.

Assuming now these six fundamental sciences to rest upon as many distinct classes of facts, we find the actual connections of those classes of facts still to be considered. And to this problem may be applied our third principle.

III. *A philosophical scheme of the sciences should exhibit all classes of facts in their actual connections as co-existent in space and successive in time.*

It need scarcely be said, that the several

classes of facts, as found in nature, are in a fixed order which is never reversed or confused. If their existing collocations and successions should be extensively deranged; if, for example, the earth should be placed abruptly nearer the sun, or teem anew with primeval ferns and monsters, the present cosmos would simply collapse in chaos. We may, indeed, within narrow limits, modify the natural order of phenomena, and take a class of facts out of their due place and time, for the purposes of a scientific experiment; or, leaving the natural order undisturbed, we may confine our attention exclusively to one set of phenomena, without regard to others that precede and accompany it, in order to make our knowledge of it more exact and thorough. Indeed, the whole scientific procedure consists very largely and necessarily in such special and separate investigations. But nature itself is not the medley that our methods might make it, and does not present phenomena to us in detached fragments. Full knowledge of them must include their real associations as part of their reality; and in a philosophical scheme of the sciences, which is to be natural rather than artificial, real rather than ideal, we must not only lay the foundation in distinct classes of facts, but rear the whole superstructure in accordance with the actual connections of those classes of facts. In other words, we must deal with phenomena as we find them co-existing together in space and succeeding one another in time. And we may obviously do this without any metaphysical inquiry into the relation of time and space to our cognitive faculty, by simply taking them as the two forms in which all phenomena are contained or presented.

Of spacial connections the most general and obvious is that between the heavens and the earth. While the progress of science has shown that celestial space as compared with terrestrial space is practically infinite, yet it has also shown that every class of facts disclosed in the heavens obeys the same laws which govern the corresponding class of facts displayed upon the earth, and that the advance of our knowledge is from the adjacent to the remote phenomena. As Mr. Spencer has otherwise expressed it: "Before mankind scientifically co-ordinated any one class of phenomena displayed in the heavens, they had previously co-ordinated a parallel class of phenomena displayed upon the surface of the earth." This at least is true of the more advanced physical sciences. Celestial physics is but an extensive application of terrestrial physics. The great mechanical laws which keep the planets in their orbits around the sun were first observed in the falling of an apple and the swinging of a chandelier; and though Stuart Mill could fancy that two and two may not appear equal to four among the inhabitants of the Dog-star, yet astronomers are showing us that the stars themselves behave with as much mathematical propriety as the angles and curves upon a slate. The waves of light and heat from the sun are the same as those from a candle.

In like manner, the new celestial chemistry is but a wonderful expansion of terrestrial chemistry. The meteoric stone dropped from a neighboring planet or from beyond the solar system brings no new substance into the laboratory; and the spectroscope is exhibiting the gases and metals of nebulæ, stars and galaxies as plainly as they may be seen in the products of the retort and the crucible.*

Even the organical sciences, as far as we now know them upon earth, are beginning to project sound analogies respecting the physical and chemical conditions of life in other worlds, as exemplified in the clouds and seas of Venus,

---

* This principle, as first stated in the author's work on "The Final Philosophy," seems to have been strangely misapprehended by a learned German critic :—" Jede dieser Wissenschaften soll einen 'himmlische' und einen 'irdischen' Theil haben. Was bedeutet nun aber z. B. 'himmlische,' Chemie ? Wodurch soll sich diese von der irdischen Chemie unterscheiden?"—*Philosophische Monatshefte.*

and the polar snows and continents of Mars, when contrasted with the gaseous nucleus of the comet or the extinct craters of the moon.

And if the kingdom of the physical sciences has already been made to embrace all celestial as well as terrestrial provinces, is it wholly unreasonable to look for a like extension of the psychical sciences? The objections to such an expectation are in fact popular rather than philosophical, and all in the face of scientific precedent and analogy. "No biologist," says Lewes, "would listen patiently if asked, what are the flora and fauna of Jupiter?" No chemist, it might be replied, would have listened at all twenty years ago, if asked whether there is any iron in the sun, or any hydrogen in Sirius? Not a hundred years since, it would have been deemed visionary, if not impious, to think of measuring the bulk, weight and periods of the heavenly bodies, as it still seems scarcely credible that we are beginning to trace their chemical constitution and climatic features; and if any of them should yet exhibit the organic conditions of psychical phenomena, through some æthereal thrill of which we cannot now conceive, this would only be what the physicist might expect as the flower of the cosmic life, and what the divine is prepared to accept on other grounds. Professor Tyndall has already said substantially that all our politics, art, and philosophy are but consequences of the refrigeration of a cooling planet whirled off from the sun; and the eloquent Chalmers, though he thought it might be overstepping the modesty of true science to speculate concerning the mineralogy and botany of other globes, could still argue from the analogy of celestial mechanics that our terrestrial ethics must agree with the celestial ethics, dominating all the higher intelligences with which his creed had peopled the distant places of the universe. Be that as it may, with this new spectroscopic apocalypse of the heavens opening before us, it is too soon to debar the celestial realms which have not yet been explored, as forever conjectural and unknowable. It will be enough to inscribe them as *terra incognita* on the map of science. That map will be incomplete without them, not merely because theoretically the field of research must be held to be co-extensive with the domain of nature; but also because celestial and terrestrial phenomena, instead of being simply collocated, are connected, and so intimately connected that together they already form one vast mechanism governed by universal law, and may yet also appear as one mighty organism pervaded with life and reason.

As to the succession of phenomena in time,

science has shown that they proceed from the simple to the complex. Although the different classes of facts are distinct and separate, yet they are found succeeding one another in a fixed order of mutual dependence and increasing multiformity, each involving its predecessor, and becoming a condition precedent to its successor; and with such actual procession of phenomena must correspond, according to our doctrine, the normal procession of the sciences. This important principle, first announced but imperfectly applied by Comte, may be easily tested by tracing it through the series of fundamental sciences which we have enumerated, as well as by showing what confusion would arise, both in nature and in our minds, if that series were broken, reversed, or deranged.

Beginning with the physical or mechanical sciences, we find them plainly preceding and supporting the chemical sciences. The phenomena of moving masses and undulating molecules occur before, and independently of their combination in different kinds of matter, and may be studied quite apart from any inquiry into the elementary constitution of bodies, and even experimentally separated for special investigation. The physicist need know but little of chemistry so long as he deals only with the forces of gravitation, heat, light, electricity which play between masses outside of molecules, or in the all-pervading ether.

In like manner, a step higher in the ascending series the chemical sciences are found to rest upon the physical, while they uphold the organical sciences. The phenomena of combining atoms, as shown by different kinds of inorganic matter, though largely conditioned by the physical forces of gravitation and heat, and often attended with light and electricity, are themselves distinct and separate, having their own laws of affinity and likeness, and are, at the same time, quite independent of the next and more complex phenomena of organic or living matter with which they have no absolute and invariable connection. The chemist, therefore, should know much of physics, if he would understand the conditions of weight and temperature under which atoms will unite to form the compounds with which he deals; but he need know little or nothing of biology, unless he chooses to advance into the region of so-called organic chemistry, with the view of studying the composition of living tissues.

And so, in their turn, the organical sciences will be found to have a basis in the chemical, and afford a basis for the psychical sciences. The phenomena of living organisms, such as plants and animals, though largely predetermined by the physical forces of heat and light, and constantly involving the chemical composition and decomposition of the organic elements, oxygen, hydrogen, nitrogen, and carbon, are nevertheless unique and accessional, having their own laws of life and growth, and can as little be confounded with the psychical or mental phenomena which supervene only in organisms of the highest class. It is true that organisms re-act upon the physical forces of gravitation, heat, light, and electricity as appears in swift-flying birds, warm-blooded animals, luminous insects, and electric fishes; and it is also true that they resist or repair chemical disintegration as well as evolve new chemical processes and compounds. And these are simply further reasons why the biologist must know something of physics, and much of chemistry in order to master the endless varieties of organic structure and function with which he has to deal; but he may remain in scornful ignorance of the whole realm of mental science, unless he cares to wander into the dim borderland of so called animal psychology in search of the germs or semblances of human faculties and feelings.

Leaving material nature beneath us and ascending into the psychical sciences, we find them resting upon all the organical, chemical, and physical sciences below them, and at the same time, sustaining the social and religious sciences above them. Although the phenomena of sensation, emotion, and thought, are closely implicated with the senses, the nerves, and the brain, yet they are clearly distinguishable from any molecular movements in the organism as additional facts of consciousness, having their own laws of association and reasoning; while on the other side, by their individuality and seclusion, they stand apart from the more complex phenomena of society. It is true that the mind largely derives from its whole physical environment the impressions which it forms into cognitions and conceptions; and it is also true that it is greatly modified by its whole social environment through other like minds with which it is connected in constant interaction. And hence it is that physiology is the proper door through which to ascend into psychology, where each may rest as sole sovereign in the empire of conscious thought and action, unless he would advance into the higher and broader region of observed thought and action, by the steps of comparative psychology, as shown in the mental manifestations of savages, of children, and of different classes of civilized men.

On that higher plane of inquiry, the social

sciences would then present themselves as the next following link between the mental and the religious sciences. As all society exists optentially in the individual, and is but composed of individuals, the phenomena of associated human beings, as seen in the constitution and history of different tribes, nations, and races, cannot be wholly detached from the individual organisms which have combined to produce them; and yet they occur in a region outside of personal consciousness and volition, as general resultant facts of human nature and human action, governed by their own laws of recurrence, inheritance, and progress, which no combination of indivdual wills, not even legislation or revolution, can thwart or set aside. The immense diversity and complexity of modern civilization, involving as it does the intellectual and moral products of all climes and ages, have indeed seemed to make a science of sociology impracticable, and some have even thought it also irreverent, because of an imagined inconsistency of social laws with the Divine will. It is to be approached through the preliminary sciences of geography, ethnology, archæology, and historiography, and should properly be restricted to the mental and moral laws of social organization and development; since the higher and final class of religious phenomena, if sought in this direction, can only be reached by a further ascent through comparative theology, in the study of the different religions of mankind.

Emerging at length, by this new method of approach, into the religious sciences, we find them at once distinct and pre-eminent. No other and higher class of facts remains, and therefore no further class of sciences. The religious phenomena of humanity, though deeply involved in both the individual and the social organism, are nevertheless themselves presented in an extra-human or superhuman region, by what the latest scientific thought defines as the Absolute Reality, unknowable and inconceivable, howsoever practically treated, whether as a mere ideal personification or as a real personality.

And thus, at the summit of the sciences we have reached a limit which divides the empirical from the metaphysical region of inquiry. But into that transcendental realm we are not yet ready to venture. Turning to retrace our steps, let us still further test the series in a descending order, by imagining one supporting link after another removed or displaced. Take away the social laws which uphold religious phenomena in history, and nothing of religion would be left but savage superstition or subjective illusion. Take away the mental laws which uphold social phenomena, and there could be no organization and development but that of animal tribes revolving in the same circles from generation to generation. Take away the organical laws which uphold mental phenomena, and the intellect of man, alike with the instinct of the brute, would disappear. Take away the chemical laws which uphold organic phenomena, and the whole vegetable world would wither away into a volcanic waste. Take away the physical laws, which uphold chemical phenomena, and nought would remain but an inorganic mass. Ascend or descend the scale of nature, you find its ranks nowhere broken, and never inverted. And the concatenated classes of facts require corresponding orders of concatenated sciences. However much either the sciences or the facts may overlap and return into each other, they still form one compact series, like a spiral staircase winding from earth to heaven.

We have seen how facts are connected in space, and how they are connected in time; but it still remains to connect these connections, in order fully to adjust the scheme of the sciences to the actual framework of nature. Now the progress of research has already begun to show that the same procession of phenomena from the simple to the complex which obtains upon the earth, prevails also, in part at least, throughout the heavens, and therefore the sciences, conforming to the phenomena, combine a collateral with their linear arrangement, embracing spacial comprehension in the temporal succession. In other words, physical science, in both its celestial and terrestrial provinces, precedes and supports chemical science, as chemical science, in both its celestial and terrestrial provinces, rests upon physical and precedes organical science. Mr. Spencer, by his magnificent doctrine of universal evolution through space and time, has unwittingly afforded a foundation for this vast serial arrangement; and Mr. Fiske has aided it, while repudiating it, by suggesting sciences of development or genesis, such as astrogeny, biogeny, sociogeny, which exactly comply with its conditions. It would be easy, in accordance with such views, to trace the successive sciences through the successive stages of that mighty development which is supposed to have proceeded from an indefinite antiquity throughout immensity; the physical sciences, as displayed in the ancient sidereal nebulæ, revolving and condensing into galaxies, suns, and planets, radiating heat and light; the chemical sciences, as displayed in the molten core and hardened crust of our earth, with its slowly forming strata of rocks and soils; the organical sciences, as displayed in the flora and fauna which have flourished and decayed, with increasing complexity and refinement of structure, until at length man appeared as the paragon of animals; the psychical sciences, as displayed through the varying scale of sense, instinct, understanding and reason, infant and adult, rude and cultured; the social sciences, as displayed in the organizing and evolving races and peoples, with their advancing arts, polities, and civilizations; and at last the religious sciences, as displayed in growing traditions, creeds, and cults, Pagan and Christian, ever struggling for ascendancy and prevalence. And it would thus be found that the evolutionary series of facts throughout space and time, at least as far as it has yet been traced, everywhere and always supports the corresponding series of sciences, ranging like mountain peaks, which rise one above another, from the solid ground, until they are lost from view in the clouds.

In further proof and illustration of this order of the sciences, let it be observed, in the first place, that it is also the order of their historic evolution. It is true, such a coincidence would not be indispensable. The historic procedure is not always and necessarily normal or philosophical. There have been great ebbs and floods of the sciences, as Bacon expressed it, with the rise and fall of empires. Man, too, is not the measure of nature, and to an intellect sufficiently enlarged or able even in fancy to free itself from terrestrial limitations and vicissitudes, the true universal order of knowledge might still appear accordant with the universal order of facts however much it had become confused in the human consciousness, or deranged by the processes of human research. As a matter of fact, however, no such general confusion or lasting derangement has taken place. The history of the sciences shows that they have actually proceeded, and are still proceeding, serially from simple to complex facts, throughout space and time. All the physical sciences have long been and still are greatly in advance of all the psychical sciences, and each in particular in advance of its predecessor—chemistry ahead of biology, and psychology ahead of sociology. The defects which Mr. Spencer has exposed in the Comtean series do not pertain to the serial principle itself, as more strictly and fully applied, and the mutual helpfulness and interaction of the sciences upon which Mr. Fiske has enlarged, have nothing to do with the question of their relative advancement in scientific exactitude and completeness. Astronomy, as a physical science, is centuries older than chemistry, as chemistry is at least half a century older than biology; and though the two younger sciences have given to astronomy the spectroscope and the Spencerian theory of evolution, yet they have not thereby overtaken their elder sister in the race for exact knowledge. It is still true, in the main, that our science of the heavenly bodies is more perfect than that of our own bodies and of surrounding phenomena, since we can predict eclipses centuries hence to the minute, while we cannot foretell the state of the weather or of our health a single week, simply because of the cumulative complexity and contingency of the latter class of facts. And judging the future by the past, we shall doubtless continue thus to master phenomena in the order of their relative generality and independence of one another. Tried, therefore, by any of the tests of scientific perfection—mathematical exactitude, theoretical consistency, power of prevision—it will be found in all history that the simpler sciences have ever led and still lead the more complex sciences as in serried ranks without a break or a recoil.

In the second place, this order of the sciences is also the order of our logical convenience. It is the true psychological as well as cosmological and chronological order. Even if it were not, we have maintained it would still be tenable as the only philosophical arrangement of knowledge. It is not to be presumed, in advance of any experience, that nature must present her phenomena to us in a strictly logical succession, adapted to our narrow faculties and modes of investigation, so that what is first and last in our course of reasoning must also be what is first and last in her course of development. Nor would any preconceived scheme of research which we might frame necessarily prove the most suitable and serviceable when applied in the actual process of scientific inquiry. On the contrary, history has developed a scheme quite different from that which men might have anticipated as most probable, and which at times they have blindly pursued as most promising. Naturally engrossed with the adjacent and impressive phenomena of their own bodies and minds, they essayed for centuries to construct the mental before the physical sciences, psychology and physiology in advance of chemistry and astronomy. But now that by hard and long experience we have been forced to follow the order of facts in our researches we can see, in the light of our own failures and successes, that such an order is supremely rational as well as natural, and that in adopting it we are but acting on the logical principle that we must master the simple before advancing to the complex phenomena, and study both in their essential dependence and connection. In other words, we have found that logically we must proceed from physics to chemistry, and from chemistry to biology; and we are beginning to see that we must ascend through physiology into psychology and sociology, and that even theology as an empirical science must be studied in its historical development in human society before it can acquire all the data needed for its completion. Thus does nature, in spite of the perversity of man, like a severe yet kindly teacher, oblige him to begin at the lowest round in the ladder of the sciences, and toil patiently upward, from one degree of attainment to another, with increasing skill and ardor, toward the fulness of perfect knowledge.

In the third and last place, this order of the sciences is also the order of their practical importance. Mere utility, indeed, as we have already seen, is not a philosophical principle of classification, unless it be in the so called practical sciences or scientific arts. It is conceivable that pure theoretical knowledge, following the general succession of facts in the universe, might proceed independently of man, or might prove wholly insusceptible of adjustment to his concerns. As it is, however, the most abstract science, though pursued only from a disinterested love of knowledge, will often in its practical applications surprise the world with vast benefits, and compel the vulgar to turn and heap their applauses upon the man whom they may have pitied as a stiff pedant, losing himself in wordy nonsense, or a mild enthusiast seeking new reasons for very old facts. Condorcet has strikingly observed, that the sailor, whom an exact calculation of longitude preserves from shipwreck, owes his life to a theory conceived two thousand years ago by men of genius who were thinking of nothing but lines and angles; and in our own day we have seen a toy-like battery in the college lecture-room of Professor Joseph Henry become that miracle of modern civilization, the Atlantic Telegraph, in the hands of the more utilitarian inventor. And upon this principle as thus guarded, we shall find that the scale of the sciences with their issuing arts most wonderfully agrees with the scale of human interests; the least important being at the base, and the most momentous at the summit, while those of subordinate significance fill the intermediate ranks. To state it differently, man as the microcosm appears to have in his constitution a gradation of relations and capacities, corresponding to the gradation of phenomena which he seeks to know by his science and to modify by his art.

The physical, chemical, and organical sciences lead up through the mineral, vegetal, and animal kingdoms of which he is the organic head and lord; while the psychical, social, and religious sciences ascend through still higher realms of human interest toward the highest of which he can conceive: and in the train of these linked sciences follow such useful arts as commerce, manufactures, agriculture; such æsthetical arts as music, painting, architecture; and such moral arts as medicine, jurisprudence, and divinity. So does science, in conducting her votaries through the difficult school of nature, reward their fidelity with ever-gathering laurels and trophies for the advantage and exaltation of our common humanity.

If we now seek for a compact result of this discussion in some convenient working classification, which shall be adapted to the existing state of our scientific knowledge, without expressing its more theoretical domains and boundaries, we may obtain it by arranging, as in the following table, a parallel series of principal or capital sciences, embracing only such provinces of facts as are now actually under scientific investigation and bearing familiar names, etymologically descriptive of their areas and limits:

	FUNDAMENTAL SCIENCES.		PRINCIPAL SCIENCES.
Celestial and Terrestrial.	Physical. Chemical. Organical. Psychical. Social. Religious.	*Physical.* *Psychical.*	Astronomy. Geology. Anthropology. Psychology. Sociology. Theology.

In this scheme each Principal Science represents, in a concrete form, the parallel group of Fundamental Sciences to which it corresponds, and includes, as its special domain, all of those Fundamental Sciences from which it is not excluded by its immediate predecessor and successor in the series. Astronomy, the science of the stars, being the most comprehensive science in space and time, embraces the whole region of celestial physics, chemistry and organics, and the unknown realms of celestial ethics and politics, together with the unsolved problems of the origin and destiny of galaxies, suns and planets. Geology, the science of the earth, as distinguished from the other planets, embraces the region of terrestrial physics, chemistry and organics, with the unsolved problems of the origin and destiny of the globe, and of the stratas, floras and faunas upon its surface. Anthropology, the science of mankind as distinguished from the other animal races, includes physiology, ethnology, philology, archæology, together with the unsolved problems of the origin and destiny of human races, languages and arts.

Psychology, the science of the mind as distinguished from the body, embraces æsthetics, logic, and ethics, with inquiries into the origin and destiny of the soul and the development of its sensations, cognitions and emotions. Sociology, the science of society as distinguished from the individual, includes technics, economics, and politics, with inquiries into the origin and destiny of the family and the state, and the development of civilization. Theology, the science of religion, as distinguished from politics, includes comparative and theoretic theology, with inquiries into the origin and destiny of traditions, creeds, and cults, and the development of essential religion. And thus the sciences tower upward to a summit, from whence, as from a mountain peak, we may survey the vast region of human research, with its remote frontiers fading into the far horizon of infinite space and time, and its nearer provinces, spread out beneath us, like cantons bounded by thread-like hills and rivers, and dotted with shining cities and villages, that serve to mark how far the works of man have encroached upon the wilds of nature.

We have at length reached a point in the investigation where some larger and more precise definitions of science are needed. Hitherto we have simply maintained that facts are the material of scientific knowledge, without inquiring into the cognitive process itself; but facts, in the course of that process, as it is well known, have become decomposed into their subjective and objective elements under the names of phenomena and noumena, the former referring to things as they appear or are manifested to our senses, and the latter to things as they exist by themselves and only in our thought. And it is now a moot question whether noumena as well as phenomena should be included within the field of scientific inquiry, or, in other words, whether only the patent laws of facts, their mere coexistences and successions, or also their occult substances and causes, are scientificably knowable. To this question may be applied our next principle.

IV. A philosophical scheme of the sciences should embrace both their empirical and their metaphysical divisions in logical correlation.

The important distinction between empirical and metaphysical inquiry which obtains in every class of facts, and therefore in every science, is as old as Aristotle, was emphasized by both Bacon and Newton, and at length thoroughly excogitated by Berkeley, Hume, and Kant. But it has been reserved for Comte to formulate it into a supposed law of scientific development under which, it is claimed, that the empirical region of phenomena and laws have been finally separated from the metaphysical region of entities and causes as by an impassable gulf, and the former retained as the only legitimate field of positive science, while the latter is to be forever abandoned as a mere realm of superstition and speculation. Whatever may be said of the truth or error of this law, viewed simply as a law of the evolution of empirical science, it cannot be denied that by proclaiming it, Comte has done a lasting service to both parties in the controversy, and opened the way, however unwittingly, to a just and final definition of their several provinces and frontiers in the domain of philosophy. Never before has the breach between them been made so conspicuous; never before have they been so freed from mutual restraint and interference, the empiricist from the wings of speculation, and the metaphysician from the clogs of experience; never before have they proceeded apart, each his own way, to so wild extremes, as for example in the systems of Comte and Hegel; and consequently never before has the philosophic mind been so favorably poised for healthy reactions towards the true, safe, intermediate position. In calling attention to some of these reactions from the empirical side, my present aim is not at all to enter a plea for the study of metaphysics, still less to discuss its methods, but simply to claim for it its due place on the chart of the sciences. If it would be unphilosophical, as we have seen, to exclude any known class of facts from the field of legitimate research, still more unphilosophical would it be to debar any portion of their reality from investigation, merely because it rests under an opprobrious name, or has hitherto seemed to baffle inquiry. No scheme of the sciences could be complete which would shut out one entire hemisphere of existence from view as effectually as if it were the farther side of the moon. Its very occlusion and mystery have been a constant challenge to the greatest intellects of our race, and the recent discoveries in physical science, especially in celestial physics, if not themselves largely metaphysical triumphs, should at least warn us that the most transcendental realms of nature, through unlooked for avenues, may yet be thrown open to our curiosity, and have their nebulous vagueness resolved into lucid stars and worlds of life.

At the outset of this inquiry, it should be remembered that Comte himself merely ignored the metaphysical region, arbitrarily and indeed somewhat contemptuously, but without erecting any cognitive theory as a barrier against it. In this reserve he was, perhaps, wiser than some of his disciples and critics. It was enough for him to restrict empirical or positive science to the study of observed phenomena, and turn his back upon all inquiry into their essential nature and origin as mere infantile curiosity or vain speculation. And he claimed to do this, as we have said, not in virtue of any metaphysical doctrine of knowledge and being, which he had framed, but in consequence of an empirical law which he had discovered, and which he applied to the positive sciences alone, without so much as examining the claims of metaphysics to any different method and procedure. It is plain, therefore, that metaphysic has suffered no curtailment or invasion from Comte other than the popular fling at it, which its name may convey. Indeed, it was his habit to stigmatise as metaphysical, not merely all essences and causes, but even such phenomena as seemed to him inaccessible because of their remoteness and complexity; and he rashly forbade certain problems in sidereal dynamics, geology, and biology, which have since been solved, or are in a fair way to solution. In a word, his whole system is purely negative in its bearing upon true metaphysics. Even though it were fully adopted, it would still be not incompatible, as

Stuart Mill has shown, with sound metaphysical conceptions of time, space, force, life, and mind; while, if freed from its grotesque theory of religion, it might even be held consistently, as it has been actually, with some of the most transcendental forms of theology. "The English positivism," says M. Janet, distinguishing it from the French, "has a psychology and a metaphysic, and consequently treats of problems which are not in the domain of the positive sciences." German and Italian positivism, also, according to Professor Barzellotti, are "at bottom metaphysical."

But whilst Comte was thus content simply to ignore the metaphysical realm as unknown, Mr. Herbert Spencer has essayed to prove it also unknowable, partly from the relative nature of our cognitive faculties, and also from the contradictory character of our ontological conceptions. A passing remark upon each of these points seems requisite.

As to the doctrine of relative knowledge, the cardinal tenet of the school, it may be doubted if there has ever been a controversy involved in such mere word-puzzles and logomachies. When Professor Fiske, tersely putting the case with so much apparent clearness, affirms that "no patience of observation or cunning of experiment can ever enable us to know the merest pebble as it exists, out of relation to our consciousness," every thing depends upon the definition of consciousness. If it simply means intellect or knowledge, the statement amounts to the mere truism, that we can only know the pebble through our knowing powers; but if consciousness include subject and object as usually defined, and the meaning is, that we can only know the phenomenal and not also the non-phenomenal part of the pebble, then the statement is very far from being true. We can know both, and the latter even more scientifically than the former. We can know, in general, the independent reality of the pebble, the fact of its existence out of relation to our consciousness, and we can know in particular, and with scientific accuracy, some of its non-phenomenal realities, the infinitesimal atoms, the immaterial crystalline forces, the insensible ethereal properties which lie folded within and behind its phenomena, and which can never by their very definition, be phenomenally manifested to us, or even distinctly imagined. In a word, we can know both the otherness and the inwardness of the pebble, the thing as it exists by itself and in itself, and among its essential relations to other noumena, as well as in its accidental relations to our consciousness.

Mr. Spencer himself admits what he terms

a "transfigured realism," that there is at least some objective existence, though its modes and their connections may not be objectively what they seem. And Professor Tyndall has most abundantly and clearly shown in his eloquent lecture on "The Scientific Imagination," that beyond the range of phenomena, and beyond the reach of our senses or of any possible microscope, there is a world of extra-sensible realities, in other words of metaphysical entities, where science still reigns in all the rigor of mathematical exactitude.

As to the other point, the ontological paradoxes, largely derived by this school from the writings of Hamilton and Mansel, it is enough to say at present that such arguments can only return to plague the inventors. If it be maintained that all our ultimate ideas of time and space, cause and force, the infinite and the absolute, when excogitated, will develop endless contradictions from which we cannot escape—this would simply be proving too much for the purpose. The empiricist who accepts these results must be content to openly build his whole system of positive science upon confessed absurdity as well as nescience, while the metaphysician who rejects them may still retain all that is true in positive science, and at the same time seek for it a more rational basis. And that the reasoning is impracticable, as well as somehow fallacious, has been conspicuously shown by its own authors, who, not deterred by the logical torpedos which they had planted in the shoals of the metaphysical ocean, have themselves sailed out sheer beyond them on voyages of the most adventurous speculation. Mr. Spencer, whilst professedly renouncing and abolishing all metaphysics, has, nevertheless, on the basis of his own doctrine of knowledge and existence, proceeded to erect one of the most imposing metaphysical systems of the world which has appeared in modern times. Beginning with the transcendental mysteries of primordial matter and force, as displayed throughout infinite space and time, he has exhibited to us a universe in evolution, from the most ancient nebula in the depths of immensity up to the most recent commonwealth upon the surface of our planet, the whole proceeding under fixed progressive laws which carry with them, in spite of all disclaimers, as the late Mr. Chauncey Wright has clearly shown, a cosmological and even teleological import, at least as much of order, fitness and result as may be seen in a poem or a drama, however devoid of mere human interest and utility. And this evolving and dissolving universe he has described as the phenomenal manifestation of an Absolute Reality or Persistent

Force, of which we can know nothing except as it may be known in and through the intelligible cosmos which it upholds and which is inseparable from it even in our thought. Professor Fiske, besides expounding the Spencerian cosmogony with great acuteness and force, has based it more firmly upon a purified theism, and done special service on the metaphysical side of theology by exposing very fully a gross form of error known among orthodox divines from the time of Tertullian as anthropomorphism, or the tendency to clothe Deity with human imperfections and passions. Nor can it be said that the value of these metaphysical contributions is destroyed by the contradictory elements which they somewhat accidentally involve, since there are those who know how to disengage them in a pure state, and render them compact and congruous with a very different theory of knowledge and being.

Besides such unwitting testimonies, there have also been open avowals in the same quarter. "England's thinkers," said Stuart Mill, "are again beginning to see, what they had only temporarily forgotten, that the difficulties of metaphysics lie at the root of all science; that those difficulties can only be quieted by being resolved, and that until they are resolved, positively whenever possible, but at any rate negatively, we can never assume that any knowledge, even physical, stands on solid foundations." And soon, as if to fulfill these words, appeared Mr. Lewes, breaking the ranks of the positivists with a flag of truce in his hand, and proposing to annex the whole extra-sensible province of metaphysics and leave the remaining super-sensible region to so-called metempirics and divines. At the same time the scientific literature of the day has become leavened with a sort of speculative physics which, so far as it goes, is simply metaphysics without the name, and as recondite as any that has reigned in the schools. "Even some great captains of science," exclaims Mr. Lewes, with the enthusiasm of a convert, "while standing on triumphal cars in the presence of applauding crowds, are ever and anon seen to cast lingering glances at those dark avenues of forbidden research, and are stung with secret misgivings lest, after all, those avenues should not be issueless, but might some day open on a grander plane." In the midst of his physical discussions, Grove was constantly coming on what he termed "the alluring paths of metaphysical speculation." Faraday for a long time doubted whether the conservation of energy should not be treated as a metaphysical question, though at length he decided to view it only on its physical side. And the veteran

Professor Tait was doubtless only speaking for the great mass of scientific men when he declared, in a recent lecture on physics: "There is a science of metaphysics, but from the very nature of the case the professed metaphysicians will never attain to it."

Inasmuch then as both the new school of scientific metaphysicians and the old school of professed metaphysicians are together entering and re-entering the trodden field, though from opposite sides, and already coming in sight of each other, it may not be too soon to look for their friendly meeting on common ground, or at least to arrange the terms of correspondence and peace. Every day, it is becoming evident, in the progress of research and of thought, not only that each science has its metaphysical as well as empirical portion, but also that the two, throughout the series of sciences, are in close correlation; so that the most advanced discoveries at length abut upon some metaphysical problem, while the most advanced speculations still depend upon some empirical investigation.

In physical science, we have been led beyond masses and molecules into a universal æther, quivering between matter and spirit, at once phenomenal and non-phenomenal, impressing our senses in sound, heat, and light, and yet itself as occult as any quiddity of the schoolmen. In chemical science we have penetrated through solids, liquids and gases, among infinitesimal atoms, so definite that they can be mathematically weighed and measured, and yet so indefinite that no microscope will ever detect them; now grouped as solid spheres, cubes or rings, and anon clustered as mere spaceless centres of force. In organical science, we have advanced through varying animal and vegetal forms to an ultimate protoplasm, composed of lifeless atoms, yet endowed with living forces; an almost infinitesimal cell, and yet a very microcosm of molecular wonders; wholly structureless in itself, and yet the source of all the manifold structures of the organic kingdom. In psychical science, we have ascended through the tissues, the nerves, and the senses, to an individual mind, unseen yet ever seeing, enslaved in matter, yet keeping an ideal empire over material nature, localized in the brain, yet embracing the remotest sidereal heavens in its scope. In social science, we have emerged among associated minds, organized in perishing bodies, yet transfiguring all surrounding nature into a new world of art; fast bound in different lands, tribes, and tongues, yet knitting continents together with telegraphic nerves and enveloping the world with instantaneous thought; ever dying, yet transmitting to future ages the ideas of long-extinct civilizations. And at length in religious science, we have risen above all finite mind, individual or social, in full view of the one Infinite Mind, invisible and incomprehensible, yet manifested in nature and revealed to humanity through all intelligible forms.

At the same time, on the empirical side of this ascending scale of the sciences, we now find a projected series of correlated forces, physical, chemical, organical, surmounted with a series of co-ordinated wills, individual, social, divine; while on the metaphysical side of the same scale of the sciences we find a corresponding series of efficient and final causes, rising from some great first cause toward some ultimate supreme end, by the subordination of the mineral to the plant, the plant to the animal, the animal to man, the individual to society, and society to Providence. And now it remains to bring these two complemental series into their due logical dependence as supporting segments of one and the same, arch; to connect forces with their causes laws with their purposes, means with their ends, throughout nature, as fast, but only as fast as science discloses them; to show that sooner or later we reach a point where, in the view of both the empiricist and the metaphysician, all forces appear as but potential in one Fundamental Energy, and all laws as but methods of one Universal Mind; and thus to trace, though as yet in part and step by step, the career of the Absolute Will proceeding rationally toward the Infinite Reason, through the physical and psychical phenomena in which it is exerted and expressed throughout immensity and eternity.

That the two opposite sections of the sciences do thus tend to unite as complemental hemispheres of truth, has long been a rational presentiment, if not an accepted result among the comprehensive intellects that are capable of including them both in their thought. Bacon, though he remanded final causes to metaphysics, and efficient causes to physics, still maintained that the two agree excellently together as expressing the intentions of Providence in the consequences of nature. Newton, while he bade physics beware of metaphysics, would have us proceed from motions to the forces producing them, and in general from effects to their causes, and from particular causes to more general ones, till we come to the First Cause, which is certainly not mechanical. Herschel thought it but reasonable to regard the force of gravitation as the direct or indirect result of a consciousness or a will existing somewhere. The distinguished naturalist, Wallace, has deemed it no improbable conclusion, that all force may be will-force, the only primary cause of which we have any knowledge, and thus the whole universe dependent on the will of one Supreme Intelligence. Professor Cooke, of Harvard, claims it to be a legitimate deduction of science, based upon the only analogy that nature affords, that the energy which sustains the universe is the will of God, and the law of conservation only the manifestation of His immutable being. As the movements of the body, says Professor Young, the astronomer, are the actions of the personality which inhabits it, so must we regard all the wonderful interactions of atoms, and masses of matter as in some way the action of the all-pervading intelligence and power. There is also a teleology, says Professor Lange, the historian of materialism, which is not incompatible with Darwinism, but almost identical with it, and there are ideal developments and speculative extensions of this correct teleology, which lie in a transcendental sphere, but for this very reason can never come into conflict with the natural sciences.

Such testimonies—and a host of others which might have been cited—are not the foregone conclusions of professed metaphysicians and theologians, speaking in the supposed interest of orthodoxy, but the careful deductions of practiced investigators, seeking in a strictly philosophical spirit, to give unity to their scientific knowledge, and find rational postulates on which to base a consistent theory of the universe. And even the extreme empiricists and metaphysicians, as they build their systems apart from each other, can only appear in the view of larger, architectonic minds, like workmen unwittingly constructing counterpart fragments of the same structure. The world may yet see the "persistent force" of Spencer identified with the "absolute will" of Schopenhauer, the aimless cosmos of Comte supported by the absolute reason of Hegel, and the conflicting will and reason of Hartmann harmonized in the Christian conception of a wise and benevolent Creator.

Descending, however, from these remote questions, we now have before us a series of sciences, half empirical, half metaphysical, arranged as classified objects of philosophical study.

PHILOSOPHY
or
Scientia Scientiarum.

Empirical region of phenomena and laws.	Theology. Sociology. Psychology. Anthropology. Geology. Astronomy.	*Metaphysical region of essences and causes.*

There is but one more problem which this series presents for investigation. It is perhaps the most difficult problem that can task the philosophic mind, and yet a problem that is likely to grow in interest and importance with the general growth of knowledge. I can do little more than briefly state its terms in the form of a concluding proposition.

V. *A philosophical scheme of the sciences should have its completion in a general science of all the other sciences, based upon their historical and logical evolution.*

If such a last supreme science be at all feasible, its high claims cannot be questioned. Without it the sciences, even if complete in themselves, might still appear as mere fragmentary masses of knowledge, having no rational coherence and no orderly progression. And to forego the search for it merely because of its intricacy or difficulty would be as unphilosophical as to abandon any other class of involved phenomena; for the sciences are themselves phenomena, mental and social phenomena, and are presumably regulated by laws which may yet be ascertained. Certainly no scheme of human knowledge could be complete which did not at least provide for this remaining field of inquiry, nor would the scientific propensity itself be exhausted and satisfied until it had entered that field and held it as its crowning conquest.

As the first condition of such a science, it is plain that all the other sciences must at least have come into being, and reached some degree of development. To attempt even to project it without such data, would be like attempting a science of those remote stars, whose orbits and periods can only be ascertained by successive generations of astronomers, or like attempting any science by mere *a priori* speculation, in advance of a full knowledge of the facts upon which alone it could be based. Moreover, science being a function of society, rather than of the individual, society itself, with the individuals composing it, must have reached a mature stage of intellectual development before it could clearly seize and solve the problem of organizing the sciences and arts which it had produced. It was in plain disregard of this preliminary condition, that the elder Fichte, in his otherwise masterly work, essayed by mere reflection and reasoning, and in defiance of all experience, to construct a general science of knowledge, which should " furnish the ground, not only of all as yet discovered and known, but also of all discoverable and knowable sciences," and which should " absolutely and unconditionally determine what man can know, not only on the present stage, but on all possible and conceivable stages of his existence." And it was one of the chief merits of Comte that, instead of following his predecessors in their transcendental search for a metaphysical theory of cognition, he approached the problem of a philosophy of the sciences through the study of the history of the sciences, as they have been displayed in all past society, as well as in the individual consciousness. Both attempts have indeed issued in acknowledged failure, but the latter was at least in the right direction, and may serve to point out the way to future success.

As the second condition of such a science, we should include among its data not only all the other sciences, but all the existing contents of those sciences, metaphysical as well as empirical, without prejudice and without partiality. History now exhibits to us, in both sections of the sciences, the accumulated results of several thousand years of human thought and inquiry; on the empirical side, an immense mass of facts, theories, and hypotheses handed down to us by seers, sages and scientists of illustrious name and memory; and on the metaphysical side a vast body of truths, doctrines and dogmas, attested by prophets, divines and thinkers of equal eminence and authority;

while of neither side can it be said that it has been abandoned by the great majority of leading minds at the present day. And until all these intellectual materials have been thoroughly sifted and tested, and their scientific value ascertained, it would plainly be unphilosophical to prejudge and exclude either class of them, or any portion of them. They are the mental and social phonomena which must be accounted for and explained in any consistent and comprehensive science of human knowledge. To offer a theory of the sciences which should ignore either the empirical or the metaphysical doctrines which they now contain would simply be a hasty generalization or induction, drawn from only part of the facts, and destined, it may be, to share the fate of all crude hypotheses. It was the capital mistake of Comte that, while aiming to trace the entire intellectual evolution of humanity, he confined his historical survey to a few nations and to the empirical region of the sciences, cutting off their whole transcendental region with mere epithets as "theological" and "metaphysical." But the healthy separation of empirical research from metaphysical knowledge does not necessarily lead to the destruction of the latter ; nor does the substitution of some new scientific hypothesis for some old theological dogma invariably involve a lasting logical antagonism between them. There are those (and they already form a large number), who can consistently hold the extreme theory of universal evolution together with the doctrine of absolute creation and find no insuperable difficulty in combining the two ideas in the conception of a personal Creator, immanent yet independent in his own evolving creation. So that even if positive science had succeeded in excluding theology and metaphysics from the whole empirical region, this would not prove that it had exterminated them or even freed itself from all philosophical connection within them. On the contrary, it would be much easier to prove from the transcendental tendencies of modern physical research, that the law of scientific development proposed by Comte, states but half the truth; that the separation of empirical from metaphysical inquiry is not final and hostile, but convenient and salutary; that a true philosophy looks forward to their reunion; and that sooner or later all empirical science runs out into metaphysics, while all metaphysics must at last run up into theology, as the highest and most comprehensive of the sciences, whether empirical or metaphysical.

It may be said, however, that a defect in Comte's argument has been supplied by other positivists or agnostics who have undermined and exploded the whole metaphysical section of the sciences by means of the doctrine of relative knowledge, and in particular that what has been termed the "deanthropomorphizing tendency" of modern science has proved fatal to the claims of the traditional theology. Having already noticed the former part of this objection, we need only add a remark as to the latter. Mr. Fiske, in freeing the theistic theory of the universe from the grosser anthropomorphism which lingers in the popular mind, has at times so nearly approximated the views of philosophic divines that it is not always easy to discern any essential points of difference; but when he argues that intelligence, volition and personality cannot be attributed to the Deity whose existence he maintains, he is plainly beyond the tether of his own premises. Until some one has succeeded in so far deanthropomorphizing himself as to take a position external to both the human subject and the divine object of cognition, and from thence to demonstrate that there is no analogy whatever between them, the mass of philosophers, with the rest of mankind, will continue to conceive of an infinite and absolute person as the true and only intelligible cause of the world. And this knowledge of Deity, though finite in its extent, may have even a firmer basis than the knowledge of other noumena which do not manifest any correlate likeness to our minds, such as that of the Absolute Reality expressed to us and recognized by us in the whole phenomenal universe. The mere logical difficulty of conceiving or imagining such an Infinite Personality or Absolute Intelligence is a difficulty which cannot even be appreciated until after a feat of most abstract reflection, and which simply transcends, without contravening, the process of our thought, while it lies in a superhuman realm of mystery where neither the philosopher nor the divine should rashly intrude.*

Without further digression into these inquiries, we may now return to our position that a comprehensive theory of the sciences cannot be framed until we shall have at least surveyed, and fairly estimated their metaphysical as well as empirical contents. The extreme empiricist will be ready to exscind from the material of such a science, the theological doctrines that still stand in the way of his favorite hypotheses; as the extreme metaphysician will in like manner hasten to repudiate the scientific theo-

---

* The conception of the Infinite and cognition of the Absolute have been more fully discussed by the author in "The Final Philosophy," Part II., Chap. 3.

ries which seem to menace his cherished dogmas; but the true philosopher will impartially retain both the doctrines and the theories under judgment, notwithstanding any seeming breach or disagreement between them, and will reject neither, while yet any available evidence remains to be produced. In a word, he will proceed to construct his science of the sciences in a scientific spirit, and from a sincere love of truth for its own sake.

As a third condition of the proposed science—and the last I shall mention—it should include not merely all the sciences and all their contents, but also all legitimate instruments and factors of knowledge in the metaphysical as well as empirical region of those sciences. Since one design of such a science should be to furnish an organon or body of logical rules of scientific research and evidence, it would plainly be most unphilosophical to neglect or repudiate any trustworthy means of information or investigation, merely at the bidding of custom and prejudice, or because it had not the precision and force that might seem at first sight desirable; and such unphilosophical conceit and partiality would become flagrant, if displayed in a quarter where additional cognitive resources were especially needed. Now, it has been shown by distinguished writers on the philosophy or logic of the sciences, such as Comte, Mill, and Lewes, that as we ascend the scale of the sciences our means of exploring them increase with their complexity and difficulty; that in astronomy we are limited to observation through one sense, and that sense mainly as armed with the telescope; that in terrestrial physics and chemistry we have observation through all the other senses, with the additional aid of experiment; that in biology, besides observation and experiment, we have comparison of organs and species; while in the mental and social sciences, where sensible observation, experiment, and comparison can afford us but little aid, we have a direct personal consciousness and recorded history of the phenomena to be investigated. But this beautiful and luminous principle, according to the same school, must utterly fail us the moment we pass from the empirical into the metaphysical section of the sciences, and begin to deal with insensible realities, powers, and principles. We then enter a region of "the Unknowable," where the human reason at once loses itself in endless contradictions, or can only grope by vague intuition or rash speculation, with no extraneous light and guidance. At the very point beyond which our senses cannot lead us, we are told that we have no other faculties or appliances of knowledge. Even Mr. Lewes, though he claims a large extra-sensible province of metaphysics as scientifically knowable, still insists that the suprasensible world is wholly excluded from the field of research, and likens theologians and metaphysicians, or as he terms them "metempirical speculators," to the hapless seekers for perpetual motion. "All experience," he exclaims, "is against you; yet if you have any means of proving the existence of an organ which grasps realities beyond those given through sensible experience, we shall admit our error; but till this is proved, we must hold your efforts to be misdirected." And he adds, that any conclusions brought from that outlying region into the sphere of phenomena, become amenable to the canons of empirical research. To all which the theologians and metaphysicians might reply: "We accept the challenge on the conditions named. All experience is *not* against us: the best experience of the race is with us; not merely the experience of a subjective intuition or illumination, but the experience of an objective revelation from the Infinite to the finite reason through both nature and scripture. And this divine revelation has been empirically verified in history, and may be logically correlated with the human reason as a complementary factor of knowledge throughout the metaphysical section of the sciences."

Let it be observed that I am not here discussing these questions. It falls within the scope of this essay only to state them as problems which must be met and solved by any philosophy which seeks to include and explain all the intellectual phenomena of humanity in history as well as consciousness. If philosophy be defined as the science of knowledge, it is plain that to determine whether there be a divine revelation, making known the otherwise unknowable, is a strictly philosophical question. It is as much a philosophical question as that of determining the validity, functions, and limits of the human reason as a source of knowledge. And in the present speculative crisis it is the most pertinent philosophical question which could engage the attention of the scientific world. We have grown familiar with a subtle agnosticism which threatens to extinguish one of the very eyes of philosophy, and paralyze an entire half of the body of knowledge. It claims to have demonstrated that the Absolute is unknowable, and a revelation therefore metaphysically impossible; and in some of the higher circles of thought and culture, it accepts this result with a tone of complacent tolerance which should only proceed from assured knowledge. But all the while it is strangely forgetting, or more strangely ignoring an immense mass of empirical proofs of such a revelation, which date beyond the earliest dawn of science, which have been accumulating for thousands of years in the view of the most piercing intellects of every generation, and which may claim to be as scientific in their nature as the astronomy of Copernicus, or the Principia of Newton. And now it is for the philosopher, from his independent point of view, seeking all possible means of knowledge in the sciences, to sift this evidence, and decide whether it is scientifically probable. He may do this, if he will, with no moral or practical intent, from the mere desire to ascertain the limits and means of knowledge, as philosophically as if he were examining an essay on the human understanding instead of a treatise on the Christian evidences. If he rejects those evidences, he will at least have certainty where before he had only conjecture; but if he accepts them, it will then be in order for him to admit the duly-attested divine revelation as a legitimate factor of metaphysical knowledge, and proceed to adjust it to the human reason as a corresponding factor of empirical knowledge in the scale of the sciences.

If it be said that our evidence of such a revelation is confessedly not demonstrative, and as yet not certain enough to serve any philosophic or scientific purpose, though sufficient for the ends of religious faith—it may be replied, that it is evidence of the same kind, if not of the same degree as that which upholds the entire fabric of experimental knowledge. It should be remembered that there are sceptics in empirical as well as metaphysical science, who decry not merely our cognitive faculties, but the whole inductive procedure of reason. Professor Stanley Jevons concludes his logical discussion of the principles of science with the assertion that the certainty of our scientific inferences is to a great extent a delusion; that the uniformity of nature is an ambiguous expression, and the reign of law an unverified hypothesis; and that there is an infinite incompleteness even in the mathematical sciences. It is also well known, that some of the most practiced investigators and successful discoverers have never mastered the logic which they unconsciously used in their researches. Yet this does not deter the philosopher from accepting the vast body of physical science which rests upon that logic. Nor does the fact that the logic of Christian evidence, though ever increasing is still incomplete, oblige him to discard that evidence together with the whole mass of metaphysical truth which it sustains. He need not reject revelation, or prejudge its contents, because its credentials have not all arrived. He may even find the internal evidence strengthening the external, as well as the external enforcing the internal; science corroborating revelation and revelation completing science, as the two ever mount together toward the fullness of absolute truth.

Let him but once, on due evidence, admit revelation as well as reason into the sphere of philosophic inquiry, and his remaining task would not be difficult. He would find that in each science and through the whole series of sciences, the two factors of knowledge mutually limit, support and complement each other—reason predominating in astronomy, where comparatively little is revealable; revelation predominating in theology, where comparatively little is discoverable; while neither predominates in the midway science of psychology, where the discoverable and the revealable are more nearly balanced. And it would thus appear, that in the metaphysical as well as empirical region, our means of investigation increase with the difficulties which meet us, and that the sciences, instead of continuing as a mere medley of theories and doctrines, may be logically organized into a system of perfectible knowledge.

With this general statement of the last and highest problem of philosophy, the object of the present essay is accomplished. We have traced the history of previous attempts to classify human knowledge, and have examined the systems which survive in our own day. The result is a scheme combining any just principles upon which they have proceeded, but more accurately and fully applying those principles to the existing state of scientific knowledge. The sciences have been arranged in a serial order, corresponding to the different classes of facts which they have themselves disclosed in their own progress. Theology, as well as psychology, has been added to the series and placed in its due rank and relations as an empirical science of religion. The empirical division of all the sciences has been put in connection with the metaphysical division in which they find their logical complement. And the whole series has been crowned with a terminal science of all the other sciences, designed for their organization and completion. Bringing all together into one view, we may picture the tree of knowledge as having its roots in logic and mathematics, its trunk ascending through the physical and the psychical sciences with their several empirical and metaphysical branches, and its flower in philosophy as the science of the sciences, while its fruitage would appear in their correspondent arts.

www.ingramcontent.com/pod-product-compliance
Lightning Source LLC
Chambersburg PA
CBHW020159170426
43199CB00010B/1103